SPENCER

# LITTLE BOOK OF
# CRYSTALS
## AND GEMS

First edition for the United States and Canada published in 2009
by Barron's Educational Series, Inc.

Created by Pinwheel, a Division of Alligator Books Ltd
Gadd House, Arcadia Avenue, London N3 2JU, UK

Copyright © 2009 Alligator Books Ltd

Author: Lia Foa    •    Consultant: John Farndon
Designer: Miranda Kennedy    •    Editor: Elise See Tai

All rights reserved.

All inquiries should be addressed to: Barron's Educational Series, Inc.
250 Wireless Boulevard, Hauppauge, New York 11788
www.barronseduc.com
ISBN-13: 978-0-7641-9590-7
ISBN-10: 0-7641-9590-5
Library of Congress Control Number: 2008939533

Printed in China
9 8 7 6 5 4 3 2 1

## PICTURE CREDITS

# LITTLE BOOK OF
# CRYSTALS
## AND GEMS

**BARRON'S**

# CONTENTS

**6** Crystals and Gems

**8** What is a Crystal?

**10** What is a Gemstone?

**12** Gemstone Beauty

**14** How Gemstones are Formed

**16** Precious Metals

**18** Precious Gems

**20** Brilliant Blues

**22** Gorgeous Greens

**24** Pretty Pinks and Purples

**26** Ravishing Reds and Oranges

**28** Color Range

**30** Pretty Patterns

**32** Black, White, and Crystal Clear

**34** Changing Colors

**36** All A-Shimmer

**38** Organics From the Sea

**40** Organics From the Land

**42** Legendary Gems

**44** Building Your Collection

**46** Seeing Stars

**47** Gemstone Glossary

**48** Index

# CRYSTALS AND GEMS

The world is full of beautiful things—from stunning sunsets and lovely flowers to amazing rainbows and pretty pebbles. While most of these disappear over time, nature's beauty is captured forever in its colorful rocks and sparkling crystals.

Salt crystals

## CRYSTALS

Crystals are everywhere—they can be found all around you. Most of the Earth is made from crystals. Some can be seen easily, while others can only be seen with a microscope.

## MINERALS

Crystals group together to make minerals. These minerals form every rock on the planet. You can see crystals sparkling from wet rocks and glinting in the sunlight.

Pebbles

## GEMSTONES

Diamond

Gemstones are stones that are highly valued for their beauty. They are usually mineral crystals that stand out for their color and sparkle, but also include organic substances, such as amber and jet.

## HISTORY

The first gemstones were probably found in stream beds. The earliest evidence of their use comes from the graves of early humans who lived around 20,000 years ago—they decorated themselves with pretty stones, shells, and bones.

The first gemstone mines were set up thousands of years ago. The Sar-e-Sang, lapis lazuli mines in Afghanistan are the oldest mines in the world today—they have been in use for at least 5,000 years and are still being worked today.

## MYTH, MAGIC, AND MEDICINE

Some people once believed that gemstones came from the gods. Many were believed to have magical powers, such as healing the sick. Gems were often ground up and used in medicines, or worn as amulets (special charms) to protect the wearer from illness.

## GEMSTONES TODAY

Today, gemstones are used in both jewelry and industry. Diamonds are used in cutting tools, sapphires are used in infrared instruments, watches, computer chips, and LEDs, rubies are used for their abrasive resistance, and quartz is used in electronics.

### ACTIVITY

Can you think of any crystals in the world around you? You might find them in your home or in a park.

Ice crystals have formed on this leaf.

# WHAT IS A CRYSTAL?

The word "crystal" comes from the Greek word "kryos," which means ice cold. This suggests a transparent, colorless, icelike substance. Some crystals fit this description perfectly, but crystals take many forms. They make up most of the natural substances that the world's rocks are made of.

## CRYSTALS

Every known substance in the Universe is made of tiny particles called atoms. A crystal is a solid substance in which all of the atoms are bound together in a regular pattern. There are various different ways that the atoms can be arranged to form a three-dimensional crystal. These are called crystal systems.

## CRYSTAL SYSTEMS

Crystals are classified into systems, which are determined by the way that the crystal is symmetrical (has the same shape and size on both sides). The diagrams below show the crystal systems. The red lines are the crystal's axes of symmetry, they are the lines around which the crystal can turn and still be symmetrical.

**CRYSTAL SYSTEMS**

There are six or seven crystal systems—some people classify the trigonal system as part of the hexagonal system.

CUBIC

TETRAGONAL

HEXAGONAL

# WHAT IS A MINERAL?

Minerals are substances that are natural (not made by humans), solid, and crystalline (made of crystals). Every rock on Earth is made of minerals.

## CRYSTAL HABITS

Minerals are only rarely found as single crystals. They usually grow in clusters of crystals, or in solid masses in which there are no individual crystals. A mineral's typical way of growing is called its habit. Below are some examples of crystal habits.

**GYPSUM**

Flat plates arrange themselves in the shape of a rose, creating a "rosette" habit.

**MALACHITE**

Crystalline growths in small round masses, creating a "botryoidal" habit.

**COPPER**

Crystals can grow like tree branches, creating a "dendritic" habit.

**TURQUOISE**

Some minerals typically have a "massive" habit, growing in solid mass rather than individual crystals.

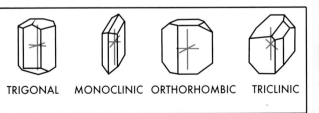

TRIGONAL  MONOCLINIC  ORTHORHOMBIC  TRICLINIC

# WHAT IS A GEMSTONE?

Gemstones are substances that are beautiful enough to attract us, rare enough to be considered special, durable enough to last through time, and hard enough to be cut and fashioned for jewelry.

## MINERAL GEMSTONES

Almost all gemstones are minerals. There are more than 4,000 minerals in the Earth's crust, but fewer than 130 of them are beautiful, strong, and rare enough to be considered gemstones. Most gemstones are made from a single mineral, although most have traces of other minerals in them.

The gemstone lapis lazuli contains the minerals calcite, lazurite, and pyrite.

Pearls

## ORGANIC GEMSTONES

Some gemstones form from plants and animals. These are called organic gems. They are generally not as durable as non-organic gems, but are equally as beautiful and rare. Pearls are formed in the shells of shellfish.

# GEMSTONE DURABILITY

## HARDNESS

The hardness of a material is determined by how easily it is scratched—a mineral can scratch a softer mineral, but not a harder mineral. Hardness is measured according to the Mohs scale. On this scale, talc is the softest mineral and diamond is the hardest.

1. TALC

2. GYPSUM

3. CALCITE

4. FLOURITE

5. APATITE

6. ORTHOCLASE

8. TOPAZ

9. CORUNDUM

10. DIAMOND

7. QUARTZ

## TOUGHNESS

A gemstone's toughness is its resistance to cracking, chipping, or breaking. Some gems, such as topaz, are very hard but are not tough so they chip easily. Others, like pearl, are relatively soft, but very tough. Nephrite jade is the toughest of all gems, but is only 6-6.5 on the Mohs scale.

# GEMSTONE BEAUTY

The beauty of a gem is determined
by its color and the way that it absorbs
and reflects light.

## GEMSTONE COLOR

The color of a gem depends largely on how it absorbs light. Light
is made of every color of the rainbow. When light falls on an
object, some of the colors in the light are absorbed and some
are reflected. The colors that are reflected are the ones that we
see. Some minerals are always the same color, while others are
colorless in their pure form, but impurities (small amounts of other
minerals within them) can transform them into other colors.

There are gems
of many colors.

# GEMSTONE SHINE

Some gems are as shiny as metals, while others shimmer like silk. The way that light reflects from the surface of a gemstone is called its luster. Gemologists use a variety of terms to describe luster.

Hematite is "metallic"

Amethyst is "vitreous" (glasslike)

Amber is "resinous" (resinlike)

# TRANSPARENCY, TRANSLUCENCY, AND OPACITY

Gemstones are also described by how light travels through them. Transparent gemstones are see-through—light can pass right through them. Translucent stones let some light through, but are not completely see-through. Opaque gems don't let any light through them.

Diamonds often sparkle

# GEMSTONE SPARKLE

The way that light reflects from inside a gemstone is called its brilliance. Sometimes when light passes through a crystal, the light is split into all its different colors and we see a rainbow. This is called fire and is often seen in diamonds.

# SPECIAL EFFECTS

A few gems reflect light in special ways—some change color, while others have stars glowing from within. These effects make the gem seem magical and greatly add to their value. See page 46 for some examples.

# HOW GEMSTONES ARE FORMED

Rocks are all made from mineral crystals, but rare gems only form in special conditions.

## ROCKS AND MINERALS

Rocks are made almost entirely from mineral crystals. But the crystals are usually tiny, and most rocks are made from just a few common minerals, such as quartz and feldspar. Larger crystals and rarer minerals only form under certain conditions—typically in isolated pockets and bands in the rock where certain chemicals are concentrated. That's why gems are so rare.

Molten rock

## GEMS FROM FIRE

Some gems, for instance, form in bands called volcanic pipes, where hot fluids once bubbled up through cracks deep inside a volcano. Many gems, such as topaz and beryl, form in pegmatites. These occur where hot molten (melted) rock called magma comes up from the Earth's hot interior. As it nears the surface, or erupts through volcanoes, it cools and solidifies to form "igneous" rock. Pegmatites are like the cream of the magma, containing concentrations of rare chemicals that are last to solidify.

Layers of sediment are clearly visible on this limestone cliff.

# GEODES AND GEMS

"Sedimentary" rock is built up from the fragments of other rocks that have been broken down over time by weather, wind, and water. In rocks like these, gems like amethyst often form in pockets of chemicals called geodes. "Metamorphic" rocks are made when other rocks are altered beyond all recognition by intense heat and pressure within the Earth. Sometimes, the heat and pressure can forge bubbles of certain chemicals into gems, such as garnets, and minerals, such as olivine.

Gneiss is a metamorphic rock.

# PRECIOUS METALS

Metals are not gemstones, but some metals are highly precious. Traditional precious metals are gold, silver, and platinum. Copper was probably the first metal ever to be worked.

## GOLD

Pure gold is a shining yellow color. It is very soft and melts at a low temperature, making it very easy to work with. It doesn't tarnish (react with air) and so it can remain bright and shiny for hundreds of years. Gold is often mixed with other metals to change its color and make it hard enough to use in jewelry. These metals can give it a white, red, pink, orange, green, blue, or purple tint. Apart from its use in jewelry, gold is also used in electrical components.

Gold nugget

## SILVER

Pure silver is a shiny white color only when it is freshly exposed to the air. It can be found as nuggets and has a wiry dendritic habit, or shape (see page 9), but most silver occurs mixed with other minerals, such as copper and lead. Silver has been used as a decorative metal for thousands of years. Today, some silver is used for silverware, ornaments, and jewelry, but is also used in industry. Silver chemicals are an essential component in photographic film.

This silver has a "wiry" habit.

## PLATINUM

Platinum is silvery-white in color with a metallic shine. It is strong, durable, and doesn't scratch easily, making it highly valued for jewelry. It was first believed to be an impure form of silver—it was not until 1741 that it was recognized as a different metal. Platinum is now regarded as the rarest and most valuable of all precious metals. Platinum is also a major component in catalytic converters for cars and is used in the dental and medical professions.

## COPPER

Some of the most ancient civilizations used copper for tools, weapons, and jewelry because it occurs in pure (native) form and is strikingly colored, so it was easy to find. It is also soft enough to be fashioned into tools and jewelry, but hard enough to retain its shape. It was too soft for blades though. Mixing in a little tin with

copper made a much tougher metal called bronze. Today, copper is mainly used to make electrical wires and pipes.

Pure copper typically occurs in branching masses or clusters.

# PRECIOUS GEMS

Traditionally, gemstones are divided
into precious and semi-precious stones.
Diamonds, emeralds, rubies, sapphires, and
amethysts were the original precious stones,
but amethysts ceased to be valuable when
huge numbers of them were found in Brazil.
The remaining four gems are still among
the most valuable.

Gems are often "cut"
into shapes—this
diamond has a
"brilliant cut."

## DIAMONDS

Diamonds are one of the most prized of all gems, famous for
their amazing luster and shine. They are virtually the hardest
minerals on Earth and are mainly used in industry—to cut, grind,
and polish hard substances. Diamonds have been used in jewelry
for centuries. Pure diamond is colorless, but various impurities can
make it any color of the rainbow.

# EMERALDS

Emeralds are well-known for their magnificent deep-green color. They are a variety of the mineral beryl and get their stunning color from the presence of chromium and vanadium. Good quality emeralds are incredibly rare—most are full of tiny fractures. Flawless emeralds are worth more than diamonds.

Uncut emerald

# RUBIES AND SAPPHIRES

Both rubies and sapphires are forms of the mineral "corundum." Rubies vary in color, from a classic deep, rich red to shades of pink, purple, and brown. All other colors of corundum gem are classified by geologists as sapphires. For jewelers, only corundum gems that are tinted deep, vivid blue are called sapphires.
The blue color comes from traces of the chemical titanium oxide. This gem has a typically vibrant color, making it very desirable for jewelry. Some corundum stones show an asterism effect (see page 46)—stars shine from within the gems.

Cut sapphire

Rough and cut rubies

# BRILLIANT BLUES

Gemstones also exist in a range of beautiful blues. Originally, blue stones were thought to relate to the sea and the sky. Aquamarine was worn by sailors to keep them safe in stormy seas.

## TURQUOISE

Turquoise has been highly prized for its intense color for centuries. It was one of the first gemstones to be mined and was originally used by ancient Persians and Egyptians for jewelry and decoration. The color of turquoise varies from shades of blue to sea-greens, and the most valuable stones are bright sky blue. As a gemstone, turquoise has to be treated carefully as it is fragile and its color can fade.

Turquoise stone

## LAPIS LAZULI

Lapis lazuli is made up of several different minerals. It owes its deep blue color to the mineral lazurite, and often contains white patches of calcite and yellow pyrite. The ancient Egyptians used

lapis lazuli in jewelry and to decorate precious objects. Powdered lapis lazuli was also used as paint and was one of the first eyeshadows! Today, it is mainly used in jewelry.

Lapis lazuli

## AQUAMARINE

Aquamarine

Aquamarine means "water of the sea" and it is the beautiful blue-green color of this gem that has given it its name. Aquamarine comes from the same family as the emerald (the beryl family) and has a similar hardness and luster. In the nineteenth century, the most popular forms of aquamarine were sea-green in color. Today, blue stones are the most popular, and many stones are heat treated to enhance their color. The best quality stones are found in Brazil.

### AMAZING FACTS

Malachite was long used as a pigment for paints. The green in paintings from Ancient Egypt is made from malachite. The green tarnish on copper is also malachite.

## AZURITE AND MALACHITE

Deep blue azurite and vivid green malachite have much in common. Both contain copper, and the two minerals are often found together. They have both been used as ornaments for thousands of years and have also been ground into powder for paint.

Azurite

# GORGEOUS GREENS

Vivid green gemstones were thought to possess great power. The French wore peridot to protect themselves from evil spirits, while in Central America jade was considered a worthy tribute to the gods.

## PERIDOT

Peridot is the name given to gem-quality stones of the mineral olivine. It is a deep oily green gemstone that gets its color from the presence of

Peridot ring

iron in its structure. It was first mined by the ancient Egyptians more than 3,500 years ago. They discovered an island in the Red Sea called Zabargad that was rumored to be so rich in gemstones that even its beach sparkled with tiny green crystals! Peridot remains a popular gemstone to the present day.

Jade

## JADE

The name "jade" refers to two different minerals—nephrite and jadeite. Nephrite is the more common of the two. It has been valued in China for as far back as we can measure, and was carved into a huge variety of objects, from jugs to musical instruments, weapons and even astrological tools. Nephrite is usually a light green or creamy color. It is an extremely tough mineral, which makes it an ideal material for detailed carving as it doesn't break easily. Jadeite is also a tough mineral, and was used by the ancient civilizations of central America who valued it more than gold. It exists in a wide range of colors—the most valuable form of jadeite, called imperial jade, is a bright emerald green.

## CHRYSOPRASE AND BLOODSTONE

Both chrysoprase and bloodstone belong to a family of quartzes known as chalcedony (see page 30). Apple-green chrysoprase is the most valued member of this group, and was used by both

the ancient Greeks and Romans as a decorative stone. Bloodstone is a dark green color, speckled with distinctive patches of bright red jasper, which resemble drops of blood.

Bloodstone

## AVENTURINE

Aventurine is a form of the mineral quartz. It contains tiny specks of other minerals that reflect light and give the stone a sparkly appearance. Aventurine is usually green, but can be brown, orange, or blue depending on the minerals it contains. It is used in jewelry and ornamental objects.

Aventurine

# PRETTY PINKS AND PURPLES

Pink gemstones are often thought to connect to the heart, and rose quartz has long been associated with love and emotional healing. Purple is the symbol of power and royalty—many kings and queens have favored amethyst gems because of their spectacular color.

## AMETHYST

Amethyst is a purple form of the mineral quartz. It was originally considered one of the five "precious" stones, due to its intense color and good durability, but discoveries of huge amethyst deposits have lowered its value. Amethysts are very common and are often used in jewelry. When they are heated, their color changes from purple to yellow producing citrine, a rarer variety of quartz (see page 27).

### AMAZING FACTS

The word "amethyst" comes from the ancient Greek "amethustos," which means "not drunk." The Greeks believed that if they drank wine from a cup made of amethyst they would not get drunk.

Amethyst crystals

Rose quartz

## ROSE QUARTZ

Rose quartz is a pink variety of quartz. It often contains tiny needles of a mineral called rutile that give it a cloudy appearance and can cause asterism in the stone (see page 46). Rose quartz is very common, but it rarely forms crystals and instead is found in massive lumps that can weigh hundreds of pounds. It has been used as a carving material since ancient times and is still popular today.

## RHODOCHROSITE

Rhodochrosite is a pink mineral. It exists as gem-quality crystals that can be cut for collectors, but it is too soft and fragile for general use as a gemstone. Rhodochrosite also forms rocks with alternating bands of pink, white, and red. The pretty patterns found in these rocks make them desirable for carving and decoration.

Rhodochrosite crystals
embedded in rock

# RAVISHING REDS AND ORANGES

Red gemstones were believed to connect to the blood. In medieval times, garnets were thought to cure diseases of the blood, and carnelian was worn to calm the blood.

An antique ring set with cut garnets

## GARNET

The name "garnet" comes from the Latin word for pomegranate, granatum. This is in reference to the most common form of garnet—deep-red round crystals that look like pomegranate seeds, embedded in rock. Although this is the most well-known form of garnet, the name applies to a whole group of minerals of many different colors. The specific properties of each type of garnet vary according to its type, but as a group they are brightly colored, beautifully formed, and durable gemstones.

# SPINEL

Spinel is most well-known for its deep red stones, but is also found in shades of yellow-orange, blue, green, brown, and black. In its red form, crystals of spinel have often been confused with rubies, as both minerals occur in the same deposits and possess similar qualities. Spinel is highly valued as a gemstone due to its high durability, colorful beauty, and vitreous (glassy) shine.

## CITRINE

Citrine is a form of quartz that exists in shades of golden yellow to brown. It is usually found with amethyst, and it shares similar habits and properties with this gemstone (see page 24). Natural citrine is very rare, and most citrine being sold is heat-treated amethyst.

Rough citrine pieces

# CARNELIAN

Carnelian is a translucent blood-red to orange form of chalcedony (see page 30). Specimens can be all one color, or form in bands of light and dark shades. When placed in the sun, or heated, carnelian changes from brown to red. Due to its color, carnelian was once thought to calm the blood and bring courage in battle.

Blood red sample of Carnelian

# COLOR RANGE

While colorless in its pure state, traces of other elements within a crystal's structure can make it appear any color.

## TOURMALINE

Tourmaline has the greatest color range of all gemstones, with shades of red, pink, orange, yellow, green, blue, purple, and black. Many stones are multicolored—the watermelon tourmaline, for example, has a pink core and green crust. Tourmaline is highly durable and has a beautiful shine—this, combined with its amazing color range, has made it highly prized as a gemstone.

Watermelon
tourmaline

# TOPAZ

All over the world, topaz is valued for its color, clarity, and hardness. Topaz is colorless in its pure state, but is found in a wide range of colors. The most valuable and rare of which is bright red. When heated, topaz can change color—colorless stones become vivid blue and yellow crystals turn rosy pink.

Although topaz is a relatively hard stone, it has poor toughness and must be treated with care. Some gem quality crystals of topaz are huge—the largest crystal ever found weighs a staggering 596 lb (270 kg)!

# ZIRCON

Zircon is well-known for its brilliance, fire, and wide color range. It is colorless when pure, and is similar to diamonds in clarity and beauty. Impurities in zircon can create red, orange, yellow, blue, green, and brown crystals. Red and blue are the most popular. Zircon has been used as a gemstone from as far back as the 6th century A.D. and its wide availability, beauty, and hardness has ensured that it remains popular today.

# FLUORITE

Crystals of fluorite form in a wide range of attractive colors and patterns, which should make it an ideal gemstone. However, fluorite is a very soft and fragile mineral, and is unsuitable for general use in jewelry. Fluorite has been carved into decorative objects, to display its natural beauty and shine. Fluorite also has many industrial uses—it is involved in the processes of making steel, special types of glass, and is even used to make telescopic lenses. When exposed to ultraviolet light, fluorite displays a special effect, called fluorescence (see page 35).

# PRETTY PATTERNS

These gems come in an astonishing array of colors and patterns. They are often carved to show off their natural beauty and their individual designs make each piece truly unique.

## CHALCEDONY

Chalcedony is made up of minute crystals of quartz. It forms when a liquid rich in silica (one of the minerals that makes quartz) enters a cavity, or hole, in a rock. The liquid crystallizes in layers that are strongly bonded together. Because of its fibrous structure, chalcedony is very tough and makes an excellent carving material. In its natural state it is white, but small impurities can transform it into gemstones that are every color of the rainbow.

## TYPES OF CHALCEDONY

Agate

### AGATE

Agate is a multicolored, banded form of chalcedony. Bands of color expand out from a common center, roughly following the shape of the cavity in which they have formed. Agate is often dyed to enhance its natural color.

## ONYX

Onyx is a black, or dark brown, and white stripy form of chalcedony. It is rarely found in nature.

## SARD

Sard is a reddish brown variety of chalcedony. When it combines with onyx, the resulting gemstone is called sardonyx.

## JASPER

Jasper is a form of chalcedony that has absorbed additional minerals, which give it its color and opacity. It can be a range of colors, from red and brown to yellow, white, and gray.

Leopard skin jasper has a pattern that resembles a leopard's colors and spots.

## GEODE

A rock containing a crystal-lined cavity is called a geode. The insides of geodes are most commonly partly or completely filled with chalcedony or other forms of quartz.

Geode

# BLACK, WHITE, AND CRYSTAL CLEAR

Although they lack color, these gems are among the most striking of stones. Rock crystal reflects the traditional image of a crystal perfectly, while gypsum has formed some of the most spectacular crystals ever discovered.

## ROCK CRYSTAL

Rock crystal is the purest form of the mineral quartz. It is a colorless, transparent substance that commonly grows as fine crystals. Rock crystal prisms have been found in South African caves dating back up to 900,000 years, and the crystal remains a popular carving material to the present day.

> **AMAZING FACTS**
>
> The Assyrians made large lenses from rock crystal 4,600 years ago.

Rock crystal

# GYPSUM

Gypsum crystals are found in a number of different forms, from silky fibrous masses (satin spar) to sandy roselike formations (desert roses). As gypsum is very soft and can be scratched with a fingernail, it is not durable enough for common use as a gemstone. However, fine selenite crystals and satin spar (displaying a strong cat's eye effect) are prized by collectors. The most spectacular gypsum crystals can be seen in the Naica Mine in Mexico—caves have been discovered that are packed with giant crystals up to 36 ft (11 m) long and 3 ft (1 m) wide!

Gypsum rosettes

# HEMATITE

Hematite is a metallic mineral, which contains large amounts of iron. It forms with a number of different habits and lusters. Due to its high iron content, hematite is mainly used as a source of iron. Ground hematite is used to polish glass and jewelry, and it is sometimes cut into beads for jewelry.

# OBSIDIAN

Obsidian is a natural glass. It is formed when volcanic lava cools too quickly for crystals to form and thus has no specific structure or composition. Obsidian is usually black or dark brown, but can occasionally be red, blue, or green. Internal crystals and air bubbles can create a "snowflake" effect in the stone, or produce rainbows on its surface. Obsidian has been used for tools, weapons, and mirrors since prehistoric times. Today, it is mainly used as a gemstone in jewelry.

# CHANGING COLORS

Changing the orientation of a crystal, or the light you see it under, can completely alter its color, or even give it a spooky glow.

## ALEXANDRITE

Alexandrite is an extremely rare form of the mineral chrysoberyl. It was first discovered in Russia in 1834. This stone is highly prized for its remarkable color change effect—in daylight, this gemstone appears green, and in artificial light it appears red, mauve, or brown. This color change is known as the "alexandrite effect." It can also be seen in the stones, garnet, sapphire, and spinel. This spectacular gem is beautiful, rare, and durable, and good specimens are among the most valuable gemstones in the world.

## IOLITE

Iolite is a purple-blue colored gemstone, which is sometimes called water sapphire due to its color. It changes color from violet-blue to yellow-gray to light blue, depending on the direction you look at it from. This effect is called pleochroism. When light passes through a crystal, certain colors from the light are absorbed. In pleochroic crystals, the colors that are absorbed depend on the path that the light takes through the crystal.

# FLUORESCENCE

When some gemstones are placed under ultraviolet light, they glow with amazing colors. This effect was first noticed in fluorite, and has been named "fluorescence" after this mineral.

Fluorite in quartz glowing under ultraviolet light

# ALL A-SHIMMER

The structure of a gemstone can lead to incredible color effects. Light entering the gemstone is scattered, allowing rainbows of color to dance on the gem's surface.

## LABRADORITE

On its own, labradorite is a dull gray color. However, when it is exposed to the light, layers of crystals within the gem scatter the light and incredible flashes of blue, green, gold, red, and purple can be seen. These flashes have been compared to a tropical butterfly fluttering its wings.

Labradorite

# OPAL

Unlike most gemstones, opals don't have a crystalline structure. Instead, they form from a gel containing a mineral called silica and water—the gel fills a rock cavity, water gradually evaporates from it, and the silica spheres, or shapes, within the gel settle into a regular formation and harden into opal. In precious opal, this arrangement of tiny silica spheres breaks up light, making the stone shimmer with different colors. The water content of opal makes this gemstone incredibly fragile—if the gemstone dries, it can crack or lose its color.

Opal

# MOONSTONE

Similar to labradorite, different crystal layers within moonstone make it seem like it is glowing. Rays of light that enter the crystal are scattered, making it glow with a pearly blue color. Moonstone is a relatively soft gemstone—it is only 6 on the Mohs scale—and so it must be handled with care.

# ORGANICS FROM THE SEA

A number of precious items are organic—they are formed from plants and animals. These items can all be found in the sea.

Some shells have amazing patterns.

## SHELL

Shells have always been admired for their beauty and variety. They exist in a huge array of colors, shapes, and sizes and have been put to many uses, from being made into beads and buttons to ornaments and decorations.

# CORAL

Coral is made from the skeletons of tiny sea creatures called polyps. It grows in branchlike formations, with new polyps adding more material to the ends of each branch. The most well-known and valuable form of coral is deep red in color, but it can also be shades of pink, white, blue, and black. Coral has been used for jewelry and carved into ornaments for centuries and remains popular today.

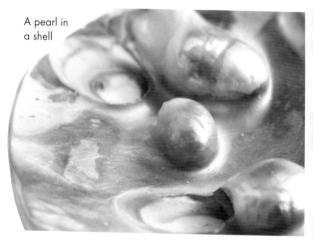

A pearl in a shell

# PEARLS AND MOTHER-OF-PEARL

A pearl is created when a small particle enters the shell of a shellfish. The animal living inside the shell covers the particle with liquid, called nacre, that hardens around it, forming a tiny pearl. Gradually, more and more layers are added to the pearl, making it bigger and bigger.

The animals also cover the inner surface of their shells with a layer of nacre, to protect themselves. This gives their shells a shimmering rainbow-colored lining known as "mother-of-pearl."

# ORGANICS FROM THE LAND

These gemstones can all be found on land or they began life on land. Amber and jet come from trees, and ivory and bone are produced by animals.

## AMBER

Amber is made from resin (a liquid made by trees) that has hardened over millions of years. It is usually a burnt orange color, but can also be shades of yellow, orange, red, and brown. When polished, amber becomes very shiny. Also, amber often contains the remains of insects and plants that lived millions of years ago.

A grasshopper can be seen preserved in this piece of amber.

# JET

Jet forms from driftwood that has been compressed over millions of years and forms on the sea floor. It is usually black with a velvety texture and can be polished to a high shine. Although jet is very soft, it has been used for carvings and jewelry since 1400 B.C.

# IVORY AND BONE

Ivory and bone are not gemstones, but they have been used as carving materials for millions of years and were highly valued. Ivory comes from the teeth and tusks of animals, such as elephants, hippos, and rhinos. It owes its popularity to its creamy color, fine texture, and the ease with which it can be carved. However, many of the species from which ivory is taken have become endangered, and international laws now protect those animals. Specially developed plastics are often used as alternatives to ivory. Although bone does not have ivory's creamy color, it also makes an excellent, durable carving material. The use of bone is encouraged as bone is more plentiful than ivory.

A carved ivory tusk taken from an elephant

# LEGENDARY GEMS

## LARGEST DIAMOND

On the evening of the January 25th, 1905, a worker at the Premier Diamond Mining Company in South Africa was preparing to go home when he spotted something glinting out of the corner of his eye. He went to investigate and dug up a huge transparent rock. He had found the largest gem-quality diamond ever discovered, weighing 1½ lb (680 g)!

The diamond was named after the owner of the mine, Sir Thomas Cullinan. It was bought by the South African government, and presented to the King of England, Edward VII. To outwit thieves trying to steal the diamond, a package said to be carrying the diamond was sent under armed guard to the United Kingdom. In fact, this package contained a block of glass, and the real diamond was posted in the mail!

The diamond was cut into nine large diamonds, and 96 smaller diamonds. The nine large diamonds, named the Cullinan I to IX are all in the British Crown Jewels.

# THE BLACK PRINCE RUBY

Another famous gem can be seen mounted in the Imperial State Crown—the Black Prince Ruby. It is believed that Pedro the Cruel, the King of Castille, murdered the King of Granada for his jewels. Among the jewels was this magnificent gem. Pedro later gave the ruby to Edward, the "Black Prince" of England as a thank you for his help in another bloody war. The ruby then adorned the helmets of many British kings and was eventually set in the Imperial State Crown where it can still be seen today. Surprisingly, this gem is not actually a ruby—it is a large spinel!

# THE HOPE DIAMOND

The Hope diamond is one of the rarest and most beautiful diamonds in the world. It is a large, deep blue diamond of exceptional quality, which glows with a deep red color when placed under ultraviolet light. As would be expected for a gem of such beauty, the Hope diamond has had an interesting and colorful history.

The diamond first appeared on the scene in 1668 when a French merchant, named Tavernier, bought it from a mine in India. He sold it to the King of France, Louis XIV, who had it recut. The stone stayed in the French treasury until 1792 when it was stolen in a famous burglary.

The stone reappeared in London, United Kingdom, in 1812, and passed through various hands including those of a banker, Henry Hope, who gave the diamond its current name. The diamond remained in Hope's family for a couple of generations.

### AMAZING FACTS

Despite its name, the Hope diamond is rumored to put a curse on whoever owns it. Several owners of the diamond have met with untimely deaths. No unpleasant incidents related to the stone have been reported since it has been in the Smithsonian collection in Washington D.C.

# BUILDING YOUR COLLECTION

## FINDING SAMPLES

Crystals and gemstones are difficult to find, but may be found in shallow, stony streams, on pebbly beaches, and at the foot of cliffs by the sea. Stones by streams have been carried downstream from higher areas and the movement of the water may have worn down the rocks to reveal any gemstones hidden within. You can also look for shells or interesting rocks by the sea or in your yard.

When you find an interesting sample, take it home and wash it carefully with mild soap and warm water. Have a look at it under a magnifying glass and write down any important information. For example, the color and size of the sample, where you found it, and any minerals that it might contain. You can also buy tumbled gemstones from nature stores.

Warning: always take an adult with you when you go looking for crystals and gemstones. Never enter deep water to try to get a stone, as strong currents might pull you off your feet.

## STORING AND DISPLAYING YOUR SAMPLES

Store each item separately—harder stones can scratch and damage softer stones. The tray in your box is perfect for this purpose. Always include a label with each item with all of the information you have.

## CARING FOR YOUR SAMPLES

Most gemstones and other items can be cleaned with warm water and mild soap (washing detergent is too strong), as noted above. Wipe soft and organic gems with a damp cloth. Harder gems can be cleaned with a toothbrush.

# MAKE YOUR OWN CRYSTALS

Ask an adult to help you with this project.

## You will need:
Hot water

•

Salt

•

Heat-proof bowl

•

Spoon

•

Small petri dish or bowl

**1)** Boil some water and pour a little into the heat-proof bowl.

**2)** Add a teaspoon of salt and stir until the salt has dissolved.

**3)** Continue adding teaspoons of salt and stirring until the salt will no longer totally dissolve in the water.

**4)** Carefully pour some of the salty solution into the petri dish/bowl.

**5)** Leave the petri dish on a windowsill for a few days. Crystals should appear in the dish.

**6)** Can you tell what crystal system they are?
(Answer: cubic)

# SEEING STARS

When light falls on certain gemstones, it reflects off tiny structures within them, creating a magical effect. Beautiful bands of light and stunning stars seem to glow from just below the gemstone surface.

## CAT'S EYES

A cat's eye effect occurs when there is a stripe of tiny needlelike crystals within a gemstone. These reflect light in a bright band that travels across the stone as you move it. This effect is often seen in many forms of quartz. This is also called chatoyancy.

## ASTERISM

Sometimes, these needlelike crystals form several bands that cross over each other and result in a star effect called asterism. The mineral corundum (see rubies and sapphires on page 19) often exhibits an asterism effect—a four-, six-, or twelve-pointed star shines from within the gemstone.

These stones show an asterism effect.

# GEMSTONE GLOSSARY

**ALEXANDRITE EFFECT**
The effect shown when a gemstone changes color between daylight and artificial light.

**ASTERISM**
The appearance of a star inside a gem.

**ATOM**
A tiny particle. Every known substance in the Universe is made from atoms.

**CRYSTAL**
A solid built from a regular structure of atoms.

**CRYSTAL HABIT**
Describes the typical shapes and clusters that a mineral forms.

**CRYSTAL SYSTEM**
One of the ways in which a crystal can be evenly shaped.

**FLUORESCENCE**
The glowing of a gemstone under ultraviolet light.

**GEMSTONE**
A solid substance that is beautiful, rare, and durable.

**IGNEOUS ROCK**
Rock that has formed from molten rock.

**METAMORPHIC ROCK**
Rock that has been changed by heat and pressure.

**MINERAL**
A substance that is natural, solid, and crystalline.

**ORGANIC GEMSTONE**
A gemstone that has been formed by plants or animals and their remains.

**PLEOCHROISM**
The effect of a gemstone that appears in different colors, from different angles.

**SEDIMENTARY ROCK**
Rock that has formed from layers of sediment.

# INDEX

Agate   30
alexandrite   34
amber   6, 13, 40
amethyst   13, 15, 18, 24, 27
apatite   11
aquamarine   20, 21
aventurine   23
azurite   21

Beryl   14, 19, 21
bloodstone   23
bone   40, 41

Calcite   10, 11, 20
carnelian   26, 27
chalcedony   23, 27, 30, 31
chrysoberyl   34
chrysoprase   23
citrine   24, 27
copper   9, 16, 17, 21
coral   39
corundum   11, 19, 46

Diamond   7, 11, 13, 18, 19, 29
   42, 43

Emerald   18, 19, 21

Fluorite   11, 29, 35

Garnet   15, 26, 34
geode   15, 31
gold   16, 23
gypsum   9, 11, 32, 33

Hematite   13, 33

Iolite   34
ivory   40, 41

Jade   11, 22–23
   jadeite   22–23
   nephrite   11, 22–23
jasper   31

jet   6, 40, 41

Labradorite   36, 37
lapis lazuli   7, 10, 20
lazurite   10, 20
luster   13

Malachite   9, 21
metals   16–17
moonstone   37

Obsidian   33
olivine   15, 22
onyx   30, 31
opal   37
orthoclase   11

Pearl   10, 11, 39
peridot   22
platinum   16, 17
pyrite   10, 20

Quartz   7, 11, 14, 23, 24, 25, 27,
   30, 31, 32, 46
   rose   24, 25

Rock crystal   32
rocks   14–15, 47
rhodochrosite   25
ruby   7, 18, 19, 27, 43

Sapphire   7, 18, 19, 34
sard   31
sardonyx   31
shell   38, 39
silver   16–17
spinel   27, 34, 43

Talc   11
topaz   11, 14, 29
tourmaline   28
   watermelon tourmaline   28
turquoise   9, 20

Zircon   29